Watching the Winners...

Learning Their Style

Text & Illustrations by Shana Gammon

Watching the Winners...Learning Their Style

Copyright 1999
by
Shana Gammon

ISBN: 1-890306-19-3
LCCCN: 99-75601

No portion of this book
may be reproduced
without the written permission
of the author

Warwick House Publishers
720 Court Street
Lynchburg, Virginia

Dedication

*I thank God for giving me
the opportunity to write this book,
and I also wish to thank my husband
for all of his encouragement, love, and support.*

Table of Contents

Introduction	page 1
Chapter 1 - Watching the Winners	5
Chapter 2 - What Directors Assume You Know	15
Chapter 3 - Budgeting Your Expenses	23
Chapter 4 - Developing Your Image	29
Chapter 5 - Choosing Your Pageant Wardrobe	39
Chapter 6 - Frequently Asked Questions	47
Chapter 7 - The Judging Panel	53
Chapter 8 - The Competition	61
Chapter 9 - Learning to Lose	71
Chapter 10 - Representing Your Title	79
Contact Information	89
Final Thoughts	91
About the Author	93

Introduction

In 1988, I travelled to St. Louis, Missouri to compete in my first state pageant. Not only was this the first state pageant I had competed in, it was the only pageant I had done.

I came from a small town of 500 people. Travelling to a city the size of St. Louis to compete in a pageant (along with 100 other girls my age) was a little scary.

Once I arrived at the hotel, my anxieties were amplified when I saw my fellow contestants. It did not take long for me to realize that I had come to the pageant unprepared and my inexperience clearly showed.

Although I had spent countless hours packing for the competition and planning my wardrobe and presentation, I had gone about preparing the wrong way. Not only did I commit several "pageant don'ts," failing to prepare properly had cost me a chance at winning, even placing at the state level. It had also cost me a lot of money, money that could have been better spent had I consulted someone who could have shown me how to prepare effectively.

I left the pageant frustrated and disappointed because I knew that I had the potential to perform better than I had that weekend. But from that pageant I learned a lesson, that now as a state pageant director, I see many girls learn each year. I had entered the pageant because I made good grades and others had complimented me on my appearance. I thought that because of these two factors, competing in a pageant would be easy, and winning one should be a cinch. But it takes a lot more than looks and good grades to win a pageant. Becoming a pageant winner takes a lot of hard work and the ability to take constructive criticism.

Each year thousands of girls compete in pageants, but as many of you have already learned, for every pageant, there can be only one overall winner.

This book is designed to help you learn what it takes to become a pageant winner by discussing topics that are essential in helping you become the "total package." Incorporating a few simple tips, like ones mentioned in this book, can make the difference between getting the participation award and winning the title.

Chapter 1 – Watching the Winners

Chapter 1
Watching the Winners

Each year thousands of young girls, teenagers, and women compete in pageants across the country. Some contestants participate just because they enjoy being on stage; for others it's the thought of winning scholarship money. Many contestants compete with the hope of one day winning a national title.

What is it that makes one girl the winner? Out of 50 participants, what makes one contestant stand out? What did she have that caught the judges' attention?

There are several factors that go into making a state or national winner. I choose to sum them up as the five "C's."

Confidence

Confidence is a key component in making a pageant winner. From the moment the contestant steps on stage until the moment she exits, the contestant needs to portray to the judging panel that she is self assured.

Eye contact plays an important part in this. When you are competing, maintain as much eye contact with the judges as possible. You don't want to "stare them down," but you do want to be able to look them in the eye. Judges don't want to pick a winner who seems intimidated when she's around them. They want someone who seems at ease and self-assured.

Often a contestant is cautious to portray confidence because she's afraid it will come across as arrogance. There's a big difference. *Confidence is the mental attitude that you have the ability to win the title, arrogance is the attitude that you have already won the title.*

Charisma

Have you ever watched a state or national pageant and immediately been able to guess who the winner was going to be?

There was something about her that caught your attention and made her stand out among the other contestants. Chances are it was not because she had the most glamourous evening gown or the strongest talent. What made her stand out to you was something about her personality, a charisma and energy that helped her have strong stage presence.

Having good stage presence is a *must* for anyone aspiring to win a pageant. Without it, you won't stand out from the other contestants. Learning how to develop stage presence involves three essential steps: 1.) Confidence in yourself 2.) Learning to take control of the stage 3.) The desire to win.

Earlier I spoke about confidence, so now, let's move on to the second step which some contestants find to be the most difficult.

When you're standing on a big stage facing a large audience, it's easy to feel intimidated. But no matter how hard it is, you have to learn to shake off those negative feelings and take command of the stage. Each time you walk out, be confident and assertive. Instead of feeling intimidated by the audience, put them in the palm of your hand. Capture their attention and keep it until you exit the stage. Be energetic and portray to the audience that you enjoy being on stage and that you feel perfectly at ease in front of the crowd.

The third step in developing good stage presence is having the desire to win. This sounds easy, as most contestants enter a pageant with the goal of winning the title. But I have been to pageants and have seen contestants who act as if they could care less about winning. On stage they go through the motions of participating in each phase of competition, but there's no excitement in their face or their actions. After the pageant is over, it's these same contestants who seem to take losing the hardest. They show more emotion after the pageant is over than they did while the pageant was taking place. To be effective on stage you have to portray to the judging panel that you have the desire to win.

Consistency

In every pageant, there are several phases of competition. Some pageants require swimwear, evening gown, and an interview with the judges. For other pageants, a talent portion may be included. Regardless of how many phases you're required to compete in, it's important to be consistent in each one of them.

Once you start competing, you'll soon learn which areas of competition you enjoy. Some contestants love interview competition but hate swimsuit competition. It's easy to avoid preparing for the area of competition that you don't like, or are weak in. However, it's important to take that area and bring it to the point where it's the best it can be.

I have seen contestants come out on stage and be strong in swimsuit and talent, then falter on the answer to their evening gown question. The contestant will talk for too long and begin to ramble, stumble over phrases, or use filler words such as "like" or "um." It soon becomes obvious that the contestant didn't practice possible on-stage answers, thus causing her scores to be pulled down substantially in one area, when she had been consistent in everything else. This is unfortunate, because the contestant could have won, or at least placed, had she practiced this particular area.

Having a weak area is normal, as none of us are perfect. The key, however, is making your weak area look strong.

Constructive Criticism

The third vital step to becoming a pageant winner is to learn how to take constructive criticism.

I've observed contestants with so much potential lose a pageant because they refused to ask for advice. They wanted to prepare for the pageant *their* way. There's nothing wrong with wanting to be yourself, you should always stick to that goal, but every pageant has different guidelines. You need to be open minded to the idea that the way you're preparing for a particular pageant may not be the right way. Perhaps the dress you want to wear for competition is too glitzy, or maybe the skirt that goes with your interview suit is too short.

For many contestants, a difficult area in which to accept constructive criticism is in swimsuit competition. When you consult a fitness trainer or pageant coach about how to prepare, it's hard to hear that your thighs need work, or that you look too "boney" (yes, some girls actually have that problem).

It's important to remember that whether it's in preparation for swimsuit competition, or another part of the pageant, learning to accept constructive criticism is essential if you want to make progress. It can sometimes be difficult, but it's worth it if you want to reach your maximum potential.

Coaching

Many contestants have had the wonderful opportunity to win a state or national title on their first try without any help or coaching. Situations like this are usually the exception rather than the rule.

Coaching does not necessarily mean that you pay someone hundreds of dollars to prepare you for every phase of a competition (although some girls do). Coaching can simply mean getting someone to help you prepare an effective talent presentation, or having someone practice mock interviews with you.

When you begin looking for someone to coach you, it's important to get someone who has *experience*. One way to find such a coach, is to ask the pageant director if he/she has a list of pageant coaches that they recommend.

You need someone to help you who knows what type of winner the pageant system you're competing in wants. You need a coach who keeps up with pageant trends each year and has the scoop on what judges will be looking for.

You will soon notice that once you tell others you've decided to compete in a pageant, many will offer to help you prepare. Although they mean well, if that person has never competed in a pageant before or had experience as a professional pageant coach, they may not be able to give you the help you need.

I have had contestants tell me: "My cousin is helping me prepare for the pageant. She used to do pageants when she was a little girl." That "little girl" is now 21, and it's been years since she competed. Pageant trends have changed since she participated, and there's a big difference in preparing for a pageant for young girls and preparing for a Teen or Miss pageant.

Getting a professional who will help you "learn the ropes," will make you a stronger competitor. Finding a pageant coach who has experience will save you from making mistakes and learning hard pageant lessons.

Watching the Pros

If you want to be a pageant winner you also need to go where the winners are. It's hard to learn how to achieve something when you don't put yourself in contact with the people who are living the dream you want to accomplish.

Learning through another titleholder's experience and observing how she accomplished her goal will be an effective tool for you as you work toward winning a title.

If you are entering a state pageant that has preliminaries, attend some of them so that you can see other girls who are winning at the local level and also meet people who are involved in the pageant industry.

Even if the pageant you're competing in doesn't have preliminaries, attending other pageants can be a learning experience. As you watch the contestants you can learn from their strong points and their mistakes.

Sitting in an audience watching a pageant is a great learning tool. So is watching a televised pageant in your living room. Take a pencil and paper, and as you watch the pageant, jot down notes that you think will help your performance. See if you can pick the semifinalists, finalists, and winner.

Pageant Checklist

Pageant: ────────────────

Date: ──────────

Number of Contestants: ──────────

Top Ten (my choice): ──────────────
──────────────────────

Top Five (my choice): ─────────────
──────────────────────

Winner (my choice): ──────────────
──────────────────────

Judge's Picks: (Top Ten): ─────────
──────────────────────

Top Five: ──────────────────
──────────────────────

Winner: ─────────────
Comments: ──────────────────
──────────────────────
──────────────────────

Making a checklist like this can be a great learning tool when you watch a televised pageant.

Write down what characteristics the winner had that made her stand out from the other contestants. Also, look at the judging panel. How many are on the panel and what type of back-

Pageant Checklist

Pageant's Internet Address: ———————

————————————————————

Director(s):————————————

Reigning Queen:————————————

Preliminary Information: ——————

————————————————————

Contact Numbers:————————

————————————————————

Comments:————————————

————————————————————

Visiting pageant websites is another way to gain valuable information on a pageant system that you're interested in.

ground did each one have? What was it that made them choose that particular winner?

Also, while you're at home or school, take a few minutes to visit the website of the pageant you are entering and the websites of other pageants that are similar to the one you plan to compete in. Most display the photo of their reigning state queen which will give you an idea of what type of "look" that pageant is looking for. The website will often include a brief biographical sketch of the winner, detailing her accomplishments. Both of these features will help you get to know the reigning queen via the internet. Visiting the website will also help you gain information about the pageant's history, the directors, and the pageant's former winners.

One of the most important things that can be learned from observing pageants and viewing pageant sites over the internet, is that you're able to see that pageant winners are people just like you. They're individuals who had a dream and were willing to work hard to make it a reality.

Chapter 2 — What Directors Assume You Know

Chapter 2
What Directors Assume You Know

Each year as I observe contestants compete, I watch girls make mistakes in areas that are obvious to directors and the judging panel. Contestants do not realize that what they consider unimportant or irrelevant to their overall performance, can actually have a big impact on whether or not they do well in the competition.

The "Look"

Before you enter a pageant, it's important to know what type of pageant system you want to enter. Each pageant system has a different "look." This look is what sets one pageant system apart from another. Some pageants are more conservative, others are more glitz and glamour.

Directors will assume that if you've chosen to do their pageant, you know what their system is looking for in a winner.

Knowing what "look" the pageant system wants is essential. If you don't know what type of image the pageant system promotes, review videos of the pageant's past state or national competitions. Also, ask past participants and state winners what they felt the pageant looked for. Getting a pageant coach who has experience working with contestants who have competed in the pageant will also give you valuable insight on how to prepare.

Knowing about a pageant system and preparing accordingly, can save a lot of time, money, and sometimes, embarrassment. Often I will have directors of other pageant competitions come up to me to let me know that they have heard a particular young woman is planning to enter my state competition. Usually their comments are something like: "You'll really enjoy having her as a contestant. She's a great girl." Or, "She has a lot of potential. She represented herself well at my pageant." But sometimes I hear comments about contestants that are much less positive. For example, the contestant came out on stage at a previous pageant with an off-the-shoulder gown with a high slit in front, when the pageant she was competing in was much more conservative.

Remember, no question is a stupid question, so if you're unsure about how to get ready for a competition and what the judges will be looking for, ask in advance!

Find Your Niche

While it's important to know what type of look a pageant wants, it's just as important to know what type of pageant is right for you.

As a potential contestant, the important thing to remember is never to try and be something you're not. A pageant system that your friend enjoys competing in may not be a good pageant system for you. As you begin determining which pageant system you want to become involved in, here are a few things to keep in mind:

1.) Try Different Pageant Systems

There are many contestants who never "make it" in the pageant world because they have set their goal at winning a particular title in a pageant system that's not right for them. Each year they keep participating, and after each pageant they find themselves trying to figure out why they didn't win. They refuse to acknowledge that in another pageant system they could advance much further, possibly winning at the state or national level. Because this contestant has her heart set on winning a particular title, she can't see that as long as she keeps participating in that particular system she may never reach her maximum potential.

If your sole purpose in competing is to win a state or national title, then it shouldn't matter to you which pageant system can help you meet that goal. There's no reason to be discouraged because you can't win in one pageant system when there's another pageant waiting for you that will give you the opportunity to excel.

2.) Glitz vs. Conservative

Determining whether or not a glitzy pageant is for you sounds like an easy task. But sometimes the word "glitzy" gives way to thoughts of fake eyelashes, big hair, and make-up that is three inches thick. While there are pageant systems that do have this type of look, the word "glitzy" does not have to mean artificial. Many high profile pageants have moved toward emphasizing how a more natural look can be glamourous.

Pageants that look for a more conservative winner can also be perceived inaccurately by contestants. Girls assume that if they were to win in a more conservative system they would be required to make appearances in outfits that would cover them from head to toe.

If you're having a difficult time determining which pageant system is for you, attend some pageants that are glitzy and some that are conservative. This will help you determine which system is right for you. Get informed so that you don't cheat yourself out of an opportunity to enter a wonderful pageant system just because you assumed the pageant was not your style.

3.) The Talent Factor

Among some pageant contestants there is a misconception that a pageant system which doesn't require a talent competition is a pageant system that's not worth competing in. It's important to remember that if a pageant system does not require a talent, it doesn't mean that contestants who compete in that pageant don't have any talent. Each of us is blessed with different talents and skills. Some girls are not comfortable doing a talent presentation on stage. There are other girls who have talents, but because they are not the typical type of talent you see being performed on stage they choose to do a pageant that doesn't require a talent segment. If you're one of those people who doesn't sing, play the piano, or dance, take heart! There are several pageant systems that don't require a talent competition but will still give you the opportunity to compete at the state and national level.

Getting Started

After you've chosen the type of pageant system you want to compete in, you now have the task of completing the necessary paperwork in order to officially enter.

I often see contestants make mistakes on applications. Sometimes contestants will complete their application half in pen, half in pencil. There have also been instances where I have seen a participant complete part of their application in print and other portions in cursive. Not only does completing the application in the ways mentioned above look unprofessional, it also comes across to the director and the judges that you completed the application in a hurry and halfheartedly. Sometimes it will cause a judge to ask: "If she didn't put much thought into her application, I wonder how much time she spent preparing for the rest of the competition?"

Remember, judges should be looking for a winner who has the total package, and this includes someone who represents herself well. Submitting an application that looks messy, especially one that contains misspelled words, is definitely to your disadvantage.

My advice is to make a photocopy of the local/state application once you receive it. Begin filling it out in pencil. This will give you the opportunity to form in your mind what you want to say about yourself. It will also give you the chance to word and re-word the answers to each application question, until you've portrayed yourself in the best possible light. While you complete your application, keep in mind that the purpose of completing a pageant application is for the judges to get to know more about you. Don't write answers to questions that have nothing to do with who you are. Everyone is unique and it's that uniqueness that the judges will be looking for. They don't want a carbon copy of someone else.

After you've completed the rough draft of your application, have someone you know proofread it for you. You should keep the rough draft, as sometimes judges will ask questions taken directly from your application, and you will need to remember how you answered those questions. Then transcribe the information onto your original application.

If you are going to type your application, make sure that your typewriter has a correction ribbon. Never turn in an application with white-out or liquid paper marks. A typed application always looks more professional, but certain local and state applications do not have room to type in the information. If that's the case for the pageant you are choosing to enter, print your information neatly in pen.

Pageant Pics

The photos you submit for the program book or for competition should always make you look your best. I strongly discourage contestants from submitting a school photo. Instead, I recommend getting professional photographs taken. Although professional photos may cost more, they're a good investment, especially if you're planning to do more than just one pageant.

When you go for your photo shoot, you should have a professional do your hair and make-up. Some photographers have a hair and make- up artist within their studio. If the photographer does not have his/her own make-up artist, ask who they recommend. Or, call different salons, explain that you need your hair and make-up done for pageant photos, and see who they suggest.

When you arrive for your photo session, take more than one outfit with you and have the photographer choose which one he/she thinks will photograph better. A good, experienced pageant photographer should be able to give you an idea of what the judges are looking for, especially if he/she has previously photographed contestants for the pageant system in which you are competing.

Having a strong program book photo does not guarantee that you will win the pageant, but a good picture does catch a judge's eye, and, when you're competing in a state or national pageant you want to take every opportunity to get ahead. You want the judges to see your photo and be able to visualize you as a state or national winner.

Getting To Know Your Director

After you've submitted a professional looking application, and an effective program book photo, you're off to a solid start. As you turn in your pageant materials and begin preparing for competition, you'll begin to get acquainted with your director. As you speak with him/her over the phone or in person, remember that your director is a person just like you. Don't act intimidated when you speak with your director, as that portrays a lack of self-confidence. When speaking with your director, be yourself. As a contestant, you want to come across as being self-assured. You want to make a good impression and show him/her that you have what it takes to win the pageant.

One of the biggest strides you can take towards impressing your director is to be responsible. Always turn in paperwork and entry fees by the deadline that your director has set for you. Before calling your director with lots of questions, make sure that the answers to those questions are not contained in paperwork that he/she has already sent to you.

As you get to know your director, keep in mind that every director wants to work with a strong group of pageant contestants (as this helps the pageant gain a good reputation), and every director wants to see contestants do their best. Even though directors want to see you excel, they will also expect you to be prepared when you come to the competition. By following the steps above, and the points mentioned in this book, you'll be on your way to becoming a strong pageant contestant that directors enjoy working with.

Chapter 3 – Budgeting Your Expenses

Chapter 3

Budgeting Your Expenses

As you prepare for the pageant, you will find that there are a variety of other expenses that will tug at your pocketbook. Because of this, it's important to determine how much this competition is going to cost.

Some contestants and their families are able to pay for the cost of pageant expenses; others are not. If you're a contestant who will need to be watching expenses while you prepare to compete, don't let that discourage you. Implementing some basic budgeting guidelines will help make preparing for the pageant a more enjoyable experience.

Many contestants decide to do a pageant and begin spending, only to find that their money is gone before they've purchased their evening gown. With no money coming in, they're forced to drop out.

One thing I suggest is to make a list of the items you will need for competition and calculate how much they will cost so you can see where your (or your parent's) money is going. You might ask: "How can I make a list if I've never competed before?" It's easier than you think! Go over in your mind each phase of competition. As you think of each one, simply jot down the outfits and items you will need for that area of competition. (*See example at right.*)

Pageant Expense Checklist

Opening Number Outfit	$_____
Sportswear Outfit/ Swimsuit	$_____
Interview Suit	$_____
Evening Gown	$_____
Accessories for pageant outfits	$_____
Outfits for pageant activities	$_____
Shoes for pageant outfits/activities	$_____
Hair & Make-up Expenses	$_____
Hotel Expenses	$_____
Eating Expenses	$_____
Travel Expenses	$_____
Souvenir Money	$_____
TOTAL	$_____

Don't forget to include hotel accommodations, meals, and travel expenses into your overall budget if they are not included in the sponsor fee. Some contestants spend all of their money on their wardrobe and accessories. Then, when pageant weekend arrives, they barely have enough gasoline in their car to get there, let alone money for food. If you begin your trip stressed, it will be hard to compete at your absolute best, especially if you're starving the entire weekend or worried about whether you have enough money to make it home.

As you keep track of your expenses, I recommend buying your outfits first, and saving the accessories and shoe purchases for last. I say this because if you have friends who have competed in pageants recently, they are often willing to let you rent or borrow accessories or shoes. Friends are usually more than happy to help out, and it's another way for you to save money.

However, I usually discourage contestants from borrowing or renting clothing. This is often more of a hassle than a help. It's easy to keep track and take care of shoes and earrings, but worrying over whether or not you'll get the bottom of a dress dirty when you walk across the stage is an added burden that you don't need. You can never predict what will happen to and from, or at a pageant. If you have a mishap, it's far easier to replace a pair of shoes or earrings than it is an evening gown.

Borrowing clothes also causes you to wear clothing that's been seen at other pageants. Just because someone else may have scored well in an outfit or gown doesn't mean that it will score high in the pageant you're competing in. As mentioned previously, every pageant has a different look. Purchasing your clothing is an investment, but if you're planning to do other pageants, it pays off.

Before you begin to panic over how much things are going to cost, let's discuss ways to help you pay for the cost of competing and the cost of your wardrobe.

Trade-offs

As you begin to compile your pageant wardrobe and prepare for competition, there are many things you will need. Sometimes businesses and individuals are willing to trade their services and merchandise in exchange for being listed as one of your sponsors in the program book. Not only will being listed as a contestant sponsor in the pageant's program book give a business publicity, it also saves you money. Hairstylists, make-up artists, and manicurists are often willing to participate in these trade-offs.

Obtaining Sponsors

In your community you will also find businesses who are willing to help pay for the cost of your sponsor fee without an exchange for services. For example, law firms, insurance companies, dentists, florists, and automobile dealers are often willing to sponsor contestants. The businesses that help sponsor you should be given a letter, by you, from the pageant director, stating information about the pageant so that they can keep it on file for their tax records. Many pageants are considered non-profit organizations and when businesses donate toward your sponsor fee they are able to deduct the amount they contribute.

Writing Thank-you's

After you have competed in the pageant, it's important to write each of your sponsors a thank-you note, thanking them for their support, and letting them know how you placed in the pageant. Even if you did not place as a finalist or runner-up, write them anyway. Everyone wants to feel appreciated, and writing a brief thank-you note means a lot to a company or individual who has supported you.

Chapter 4 – Developing Your Image

Chapter 4
Developing Your Image

Once you decide to enter a pageant, you will see that developing and maintaining a proper physical appearance for competition can be one of the most difficult challenges a pageant contestant will face. It's all about developing an image that's right for you, and learning to do this is something that starts months before pageant competition.

As you work on developing your image and your figure, it's important to remember that everyone has their own special look. Each of us has flaws and things about our body that we would like to change. Learning to be confident and happy with the way you look (even those flaws) helps you not only become a stronger pageant contestant, but, most importantly, a better person.

The key to maintaining yourself physically for pageant competition is learning how to look your best from head to toe.

Hair

Prior to competition, consult your personal hair stylist about how to properly care for your hair. Always avoid excessive washing and drying. If you will be tanning for competition and exposing your hair to lots of sun, ask your hairstylist which products he/she would recommend that will help keep your hair in great shape.

Some cosmetologists offer a special type of treatment called a "glosser" which gives your hair a shiny, healthy look. This treatment is something I highly recommend.

Conditioning treatments are also a good idea no matter what time of year you're competing. Even if you're competing in a pageant during a season when your hair hasn't been exposed to harsh weather, it's still to your advantage to have conditioning treatments.

If you have trouble styling your hair, you may want to consider getting a hairstylist to help you backstage. (However, keep in mind that some pageants won't allow make-up artists and hair stylists backstage.) If you can't get someone to help you, call a salon that's located in the town you're competing in. Explain that you need to get your hair done for a pageant, and when booking the appointment, make sure the hair stylist allows enough time to style your hair so that you won't miss any of the pageant activities.

If you are not allowed to have a hairstylist with you backstage and are not able to schedule an appointment with a hairstylist in the area where you will be competing, consult your personal hairstylist prior to the competition and have him/her teach you ways to style your hair for competition. Practice these styles with your hairdresser until you feel comfortable doing them yourself.

Remember, always go with a hair style that looks natural for you. The weekend of competition is not a good time to experiment with a new hair color or a radical new style.

The Eyes

As you compete, you have the opportunity to express many emotions to the judging panel, not just through the words you speak, but also through eye contact.

Because of this, one of the biggest pageant "don'ts" is don't wear glasses for competition. They detract from your facial features and don't show well under the bright lights of the stage. Investing in a pair of contact lenses (if you don't already own some) is best. If you will be wearing contact lenses when you compete and have never worn them, don't wait until competition weekend to try them out. If your eyes are sensitive, they may become irritated from your new lenses. Having red, puffy eyes is the last thing you want the judges to see.

There are some contestants who choose to wear colored or tinted contact lenses for competition. I think that looking as natural as possible is always best, but if you have your heart set on getting colored lenses for the pageant, try getting some lenses that will enhance your natural color, rather than change it completely.

Your local eye doctor, or optician, will be able to show you the variety of colors the lenses come in, and will be able to help you select the color that looks best on you.

Your Smile

Even though you smile several times during the day, it's hard to remember to smile when you're in front of a judging panel and an audience. But if you forget to smile when you're on stage, your scores will definitely suffer.

One way to perfect your smile is to practice in front of the mirror. Remember to keep your smile looking natural. Then, practice smiling and walking on stage at the same time. It may seem silly, but if you get into a routine of doing this, when competition comes it will seem easy.

During the pageant, don't turn your smile on in front of the judges, and off when you think they can't see you. This looks "robotic" and a forced smile makes you look insincere and uncomfortable on stage.

No matter how much you practice or how many times you smile while on the stage, you can't have a winning smile if your teeth don't look their absolute best. Some contestants choose to have their teeth cosmetically whitened. This can be expensive and some dentists don't perform the procedure. Your dentist should be able to give you an estimate of what it would cost to have your teeth whitened, and should be able to refer you to someone if he/she does not do cosmetic dentistry.

If having your teeth professionally whitened is not in your budget, prior to competition, use a toothpaste that contains a whitening agent.

Skin

Taking care of your skin should always be a part of your daily routine. As pageant time draws near, you'll find that tak-

As you work on developing your image and your figure, it's important to remember that everyone has their own special look.

ing time to take care of your skin (along with everything else) will be a challenge.

One important factor to maintaining healthy looking skin is to drink lots of water. This will not only help purify your system, it also helps purify your skin, enabling it to flush out impurities that can often lead to blemishes. Drinking water is also important if you're planning to tan for competition. Your body needs extra fluids to make up for the fluids that it loses to perspiration.

If you choose to tan for competition, avoid "crash tanning," meaning, avoid tanning for long periods of time just a few days before competition. This can cause your skin to burn, look blotchy, and possibly break out. Regulate your tanning time, and, if at all possible, tan in natural sunlight. In order to prevent your skin from becoming dry due to sun exposure, use a moisturizing lotion, preferably one that contains aloe vera.

If you will be using a tanning creme, practice applying the creme several days before competition. Applying the creme unevenly will cause you to have streaks of color on your skin.

Your Body

For girls and young women who have always been blessed with being thin, it's hard to get used to the idea of watching the diet and exercising regularly. For contestants who have always struggled with their weight, the task is even harder.

Regardless of whether or not you're overweight, it's important to be toned for competition. Being toned helps keep thighs and other parts of your body from jiggling on stage. Looking out of shape can cause you to lose points in competition, and sometimes those points can make a big difference in whether or not you win, or even place in the pageant.

Consulting a fitness trainer is a great way to determine which exercises will help you get toned for competition. A fitness trainer who has helped coach pageant contestants will be able to give you an honest opinion on what the judges will expect to see in swimwear/sportswear competition. Fitness trainers can also serve as a support system for you by monitoring your progress and encouraging you as your body gets in shape. (You should definitely consult a fitness trainer before you start incorporating weights into your exercise routine.)

Another way to tone your body is by walking or running. Both are a great way to relieve stress – which is something that you'll learn a lot about when preparing for a pageant.

As you prepare physically for a pageant, it's also important to remember that the food you eat plays an important part in your overall appearance. If you are a self-declared "junk food queen," it will show through. If you don't know how to incorporate a diet that's right for you, consult a dietician, or your physician.

Looking good takes time. Crash diets and hard exercise a few days before the pageant are never a good idea. Pace yourself by eating right and exercising. Before you know it, the fear of not fitting into your swimsuit will be a thing of the past.

The Walk

Another factor in developing your overall image is learning how to walk. Easy, right? You've been doing that for years! Unfortunately, over the years, it's easy to develop poor walking habits. The little things, like walking with your shoulders back and your back straight are extremely important. It's hard to convince a judging panel that you have confidence in yourself and confidence to represent a title, when you walk with your shoulders hunched. That sends a signal of insecurity.

If possible, find a pageant coach that will help critique your walk. Also, certain pageant systems have a different type of walk that they look for. Some pageants have a more conservative walk, while others like to see more of a model/runway look. A pageant coach can help you in developing a walk that's right for you and the pageant you're competing in.

Make-Up

Some contestants choose to bring a make-up artist with them backstage. Certain pageant systems don't allow this, which is one reason why I recommend learning to do your own make-up.

Prior to competition, I suggest consulting a make-up artist to see which colors look right on you. You may wish to have him/her show you the correct way to apply the make-up and any make-up "tricks" which would help enhance your look. By practicing these application techniques prior to competition, you'll feel comfortable doing your own make-up when pageant time comes.

Remember that your make-up should always look as natural as possible. On stage you want to enhance and darken your make-up from what you wear during the day, but colors and application should never look gaudy. Avoid using dark lipsticks, blushers, and eye make-up that could cause you to look too "harsh" on stage. As with your hairstyle, it's important to remember that the time of state competition is not a good time to experiment. Using new make-up brands and colors that you're not used to prior to going in for interview, or going out on stage, is not a good idea.

Manicures

Getting your nails manicured for competition should be on every contestant's list of things to do prior to competition.

Often, contestants will come to a competition with nails that are too short, too long, or the wrong color. Their nails don't have a good shape and sometimes they're clipped in a way that makes them look too squared.

In pageants, the little things often make a big difference, and believe it or not, the judges do notice your nails.

When you go to have your nails done, it's usually best to have them done in a nude color or a french manicure, as this looks more natural. Never get your nails painted in a color that matches your pageant clothes, as you don't want to draw attention to your hands. I encourage contestants to have their nails manicured at least a couple of days prior to competition, especially if they're going to have artificial nails or tips applied. If you've never worn artificial nails, you need at least a day, preferably two, to get used to them. You'll see that your daily routine of putting on make-up, putting in contact lenses, and even getting dressed, will be awkward with your new long nails.

While you're at the salon, you may want to ask the manicurist how to fix a nail if it chips or breaks during pageant weekend.

Waxing

Waxing is another service that many contestants choose to have done prior to competition. Waxing can give you a smoother look and saves you the hassle of shaving. Waxing can be an uncomfortable procedure which is why some contestants choose not to have it done.

I suggest getting your eyebrows waxed first. Then, if you find having your eyebrows waxed is too painful, you probably want to avoid getting your legs, or your bikini line waxed.

Facials

Of all the parts of your body, your facial skin is the area which takes the brunt of sun and wind exposure. Getting a facial prior to competition is a great way to keep your skin looking healthy. Facials aid in removing dirt that causes clogged pores, which ultimately results in blemishes.

If you can't afford to have a facial done professionally, there are several companies that offer excellent facials which can be purchased over the counter.

As you've read this chapter, have you been wondering how you're ever going to get it together in time for competition? Even though it seems as if there are a million things to do (and there are), hard work always pays off, and eventually everything will come together. Remember to relax, not get stressed out, and in the midst of everything, make preparing for the pageant a fun and positive experience, because before you know it, it will all be over.

Chapter 5 – Choosing Your Pageant Wardrobe

Chapter 5
Choosing Your Pageant Wardrobe

Choosing which clothing you will wear for pageant competition can be both fun and exciting. Even though you may find choosing your outfits to be a little stressful, it's still a "fun" kind of stress.

Before You Shop

Before you "hit the stores," it's a good idea to make a list of the outfits you will need. Include everything, such as shoes, bras, and accessories, so that you don't have to make numerous trips to the same shop.

Another thing that I suggest before you go to the store, is to fix your hair and make-up similar to the way you will be wearing it for competition. It's difficult to get an idea of how an outfit is going to look on you during competition when you're trying it on without your make-up, and your hair is in a ponytail. You'll be surprised at how these little things make a big difference in how an outfit looks on you.

Some contestants will also have a color analysis done to see which colors look best on them and which colors they should avoid wearing. If you're able to have this done, I do recommend it, especially before you purchase your clothing. Knowing which colors look best on you will save a lot of time when you're shopping for your pageant wardrobe.

Where to Shop

One of the most important steps you take when purchasing your pageant clothing is selecting a store that will meet your needs. You need to choose a pageant or formal wear store that has experience fitting pageant winners. The store personnel or seamstress should be knowledgeable in what the major pageant systems are looking for. They should be concerned with

When shopping, choose a store that has experience in clothing pageant winners.

wardrobing you in clothing that will help you win, instead of trying to sell you something with a hefty price tag. Purchasing pageant clothing is an investment and you want it to be right.

I suggest asking your pageant director which stores he/she recommends. Also, look through different pageant magazines which will list stores in your area that sell pageant wear. Some of these stores will list the names of pageant winners they've clothed for competition.

If you have a pageant coach, take him or her with you so that they can give their opinion on what looks best on you and whether or not the outfit(s) will be acceptable for the pageant you'll be competing in.

After you've selected a store, now comes the task of picking out what you're going to wear. As you look through the dozens of evening gowns and try on various interview suits, there are some basic guidelines you should follow. Let's look at four important areas to consider when purchasing your pageant clothing.

Color

As mentioned before, some contestants choose to have a color analysis done to help them determine what colors they should or shouldn't wear. If this is not in your budget, there are several books you can purchase or check out from the library that will help you know which colors complement you the most. The colors that look best on you are determined by your hair, skin tone, and eye color. Even though you may be fair skinned and plan on tanning for competition, the colors that fit into your color scheme should still be the same.

After you have determined your "color palette," you should then ask yourself the following questions: 1.) "Which of these colors do I feel most comfortable in?" 2.) "Which of these colors give me the most confidence?" Once these questions have been answered, you'll know exactly which colors to look for when you go shopping.

You may notice or hear another contestant mention that they plan to go with a color theme when purchasing their pageant outfits. For example, they may choose to wear white for every phase of competition. I recommend showing more of a variety. Bring out your personality and let the judges get to know you. For example, if you find a swimsuit in a color that looks good on you, and gives you confidence, buy it! It doesn't matter if you're the only one wearing that color, if it looks flattering and falls within pageant guidelines, don't be afraid to purchase it.

Body Type

Your body type will play an important role in the type of clothing you select. Some girls have more straight/defined body lines while others have body lines that are more curved. There's no "right" or "wrong" body type. The key is to determine your body line and which outfits are going to flatter you the most. A sales clerk with experience in the fashion industry, and experience in fitting pageant winners can help you choose garments that complement your figure.

Keep in mind when you try on different articles of clothing that there will be styles that you won't be able to wear because of the shape of your body. Instead of trying to force yourself into something, choose an outfit that's more suited for your figure. For example, you may have a desire to wear a two-piece swimsuit, but because of your shape, that particular style may not look as flattering on you as a one-piece. So often contestants think that the more they show of their body, the more it will appear to the judges that they're physically fit. However, if their body shape is not suited for a two-piece, their scores will drop instead of rise. If your desire is to win the pageant (and chances are it is), making small concessions, such as wearing a one-piece instead of a two-piece, are worth it.

Design/Style

The design and style of a garment can drastically affect how an outfit will look on you. Even though you may not realize it, a simple piece of clothing in a certain design can make your hips seem large, your thighs look "thick," or your chest appear small. As you try on different garments, you'll see which outfits flatter you the most.

One thing that I suggest to contestants is to avoid purchasing clothing that has a heavy print to it, such as florals, polka dots, etc. Heavily printed garments make a loud statement, and even though you want to stand out from the other contestants, you want the judges to remember you as a person and not for the clothes you wear.

Fit/Length

As you purchase your pageant clothing, it's important to make sure that your clothes fit. It sounds simple, but it's something that many contestants don't do. Just because an outfit you take off the rack is supposed to be your size, it doesn't mean that the garment doesn't need a few alterations. For example, you may find an evening gown that technically "fits," but it might need an inch or two taken in through the shoulders. Alterations such as this make a big difference. Remember, the judges will be critiquing the look *and* fit of your garments so it's important to wear clothing that is tailored to fit in every area.

The length of your clothing is also important. I have seen so many contestants come out on stage with an evening gown or talent dress that is either too short or too long. Often it's because when they went to purchase the outfit, they didn't try it on with the shoes they were planning to wear with it. Standing barefoot in the store's dressing room, the length of the gown looked fine, but when they put on their three-inch heels for competition, it changed the length of the gown dramatically. If you haven't purchased your shoes for competition prior to when you decide to go clothes shopping, ask the salesclerk if you may borrow a pair with a similar heel to try on with your outfits, or take a pair with you that have the same size heel.

Appearance & Presentation

After you purchase your clothing, be sure to take your pageant wear to the local dry cleaners before you leave for competition. I have seen contestants wear evening gowns that looked like they had been stored in an evening gown bag for several weeks. Presentation is important. Having your clothes steamed and pressed professionally is an extra expense, but it's worth it.

Chapter 6 – Frequently Asked Questions

Chapter 6
Frequently Asked Questions

Throughout this book I've tried to cover the major topics that contestants encounter when preparing for a pageant competition. But no matter how many subjects you address, there will always be more questions that contestants have. Before we move on to talk about competition and the judging panel, I wanted to take a chapter and devote it to a few of the questions that I'm frequently asked.

"Are judges influenced by crowd support?"

Even though a judging panel shouldn't be swayed by how many "fans" you have in the audience, I believe that judges are often influenced by crowd support. When this happens I think it's because they want to pick a winner that they believe the audience likes and supports.

I encourage contestants to bring as many people as possible to their competition. If the pageant allows, have your group make signs with your name on them to wave during the pageant. Having several people in the audience who are cheering for you will also bolster your confidence when you are on stage.

"One of the contestants I will be competing against was the first runner-up in last year's pageant. I heard that the first runner-up is usually favored to win if she comes back to compete. Is this true?"

Sometimes when a contestant hears that last year's first runner-up is entering the pageant again, she will let that discourage her from competing and will even decide to drop out.

Receiving a position as first runner-up should never be discredited, but you also need to realize that last year's pageant *was* last year's pageant. This year there will be a different judging panel, and different panels look for different things.

I have seen contestants who received first runner-up honors use the next twelve months to prepare even harder for next year's competition. They used the experience of placing first runner-up as a building block and learning experience to help them become a better contestant. I have also watched other contestants fail to prepare for next year's pageant because they assumed that since they placed first runner-up last year they would win the competition if they chose to compete again.

One important lesson to learn when you start competing is that you are your own competition. If you go into a pageant intimidated by another contestant or contestants, you won't be able to do your best. Concentrate on *your* goals and what *you* need to work on. Worrying over your competition will only blur your focus and keep you from competing at your maximum level.

"My director sent me some information about program book ads. Is selling ads for the program book necessary?"

I encourage contestants to sell ads for the program book because it increases their "marketability." Often judges receive a copy of the program book prior to the pageant, so you want the judges to come to the competition with your name on their mind. That's difficult to do when you have your one small photo lined up with everyone else's in the contestants' photo page. By having your name and photo put in ads, it helps you gain name and face recognition with the judges.

When you turn in your ads, make certain that they are professionally done. Don't turn in ads that have been hand-drawn or handwritten.

"I'm getting ready to purchase my pageant clothing but I'm having a difficult time deciding which accessories I should choose. When it comes to jewelry, how much is too much?"

Accessories should complement your outfits, not detract from them. I suggest avoiding large earrings for interview and swimsuit competition. Large sized earrings should be reserved for your evening gown, but remember, they need to look complementary and not gaudy.

Another thing that I recommend is not to wear numerous rings. Some girls love to wear several rings, but when you're competing, try to limit it to no more than two.

As for necklaces and bracelets, I would recommend those for evening gown and talent competition only, and then it would depend on the style of your evening gown.

"Someone told me that you can't go wrong by purchasing a white evening gown. Is this true?"

No. Even though white is a wonderful evening gown color and you frequently see winners wearing white, white is not for everyone. Some girls who have light colored hair and are fair skinned look "washed out" in a white gown. If white is not for you, don't despair. There has been many a pageant winner who has won her title in a gown that wasn't white.

"When I purchase my shoes, what type should I purchase to wear with my swimsuit?"

Some pageants will ask you to wear a certain type of shoe with your swimsuit. Whether you're to wear sandals or high heels, I recommend wearing a color that doesn't draw attention to your feet. I suggest getting shoes that blend with your skin tone. If you're wearing high heels with your swimsuit, choose some in a taupe color or acrylic. Wearing shoes that blend with your skin color elongates the look of your legs.

"I'm getting ready to compete in my first pageant. The thought of getting up on stage scares me. I'm afraid that when the time comes I won't be able to go through with it."

Many a contestant has experienced stage fright. However, the good news is that for most contestants, the things that they fear will happen to them on stage never come true. Try to relax, focus on your performance, and if another contestant needs help backstage, try to lend a helping hand. All of these things will help you get your mind off of those "stage jitters" and make the pageant a more enjoyable experience.

Chapter 7 – The Judging Panel

Chapter 7
The Judging Panel

The thought of the judging panel is a thought that is often put in the back of a contestant's mind. Even though they know all of their hard work has been aimed at doing the things that will impress the panel, and that this group will determine who walks away with the title, it's not until they find themselves looking at the judging panel in the interview room, or from the stage, that the judges actually become a reality. You see them for the first time as people, individuals who are watching you and evaluating you. Scary, isn't it?

But as you prepare to compete, remember that the judges are just people. They deserve your respect, but you shouldn't be intimidated by them. They're looking for a winner who's confident, not insecure. You'll see that this is a group of individuals from different walks of life, each one with their own likes and dislikes, and each one with their own opinion of who should win the competition.

Before you compete, it's important to understand who the judges are, how they will judge, and what you can do to get them on your side.

Their Job

If you think that judging a pageant is an easy job, think again. It's not a glamourous position to be in, instead, it's one that takes a lot of hard work.

A judge spends pageant weekend critiquing and scoring one contestant after another. They're trying hard to pick someone who fits the description of what the pageant is looking for, while trying to give each participant their full attention. It can be stressful for a judge. Don't think that just because they're sitting on the "other side" they have it easy.

Who Are They?

Sometimes contestants get flustered during competition because they think a judge doesn't like them, and therefore, they get discouraged and think that they've lost any chance they had at winning. This is typically not the case. These assumptions are usually caused because the contestant was not used to the judge's personality, and, under the stress of competition, the contestant perceived the judge's reactions to be worse than they were.

It's also important to remember that the judges have been asked by the pageant organization and the director to do a job - pick the contestant who they feel best represents what the pageant is looking for. The pageant will expect them to act as professionals and you should want them to do the same. Acting professional and being impersonal are two different things.

Occasionally you will have a judge that likes to be perceived as intimidating, just to see how contestants will stand up under the pressure, but this is not the norm. If you should encounter a judge like this, don't let his/her personality distract you. Remember to be yourself and do your best.

How They Score

A quick scan of your program book will show you that the judges are a diverse group of people. Because of this, each judge is going to look at a contestant differently. For example, a judge who works as a journalist will probably favor a contestant who has strong communication skills. He/she may not take off as many points for a slight error in a turn as they would an answer that is not expressed well. Their "comfort zone" is communications, not the intricacies of pageantry. This doesn't mean that if you did make a mistake in your walk or turns that they wouldn't deduct points. It means that each judge has his own area of expertise. Knowing that area and understanding how that will affect their perception will help you a great deal.

Even though each judge has a different professional background, there are mistakes that contestants will make, resulting in deductions from each member of the panel. I've discussed some of these mistakes already, but now let's look at each phase of competition and how these mistakes can affect your scores.

Interview

1.) *Not knowing the answer to a question or not articulating the answer well*
Solution: Stay informed on current events by reading the paper, watching television, or listening to the radio. Have your friends and family members ask you questions at different times during the day or evening so that you get used to answering questions spontaneously.

2.) *Eye contact*
Solution: As your friends and family ask you questions, make sure that you look them in the eye when giving your answers. This will help you get practice at maintaining good eye contact.

3.) *Voice Projection*
Solution: Being soft spoken can sometimes appear to the judges as if you're insecure. If you are soft spoken, practice answering questions in a louder tone. Of course, you don't want to yell, but you do want the judges to hear you.

4.) *Posture*
Solution: This can include slouching if you're having a one-on-one interview, or slumping if you're standing in front of the judges. Practicing good posture at home and at school is the best way to break any bad posture habits you may have learned along the way. If you're standing in interview, stand with your back straight and shoulders back. If you're sitting, sit with your back straight. Don't cross your legs; instead, cross your ankles.

5.) *Grooming*
   Solution: In interview, judges will deduct for excessive make-up, messy hairstyle, and if your clothes do not fit properly (ex: skirts that are too short or tight, jackets that are too baggy). They will also deduct for nails that are painted in loud colors and accessories that are too flamboyant (ex: big bracelets, large earrings).

Swimsuit

1.) *Physical fitness*
   Solution: Years ago, the swimsuit portion was just another part of the competition. But in recent years more of an emphasis has been placed on physical fitness. Now you need to look fit in your swimsuit. Your body should be toned, not flabby. Consulting a fitness trainer who can help you develop a workout/exercise routine is the key. Developing a good diet is also important.

2.) *Walk and posture*
   Solution: Having a good walk and performing good turns is essential, especially in the area of swimsuit competition, where you have nothing to hide shaky knees (or anything else for that matter). Because the judges can see so much of you, slouching, slumping, and walking stiffly stand out terribly in swimsuit competition. Again, practicing your walk and posture at home or in front of your pageant coach is the best way to overcome poor habits.

3.) *Color, fit, and style of swimsuit*
   Solution: As mentioned earlier in the book, it's important to choose a swimsuit in a color that is flattering. Judges will also look at how your swimsuit fits and how the style looks on you.

4.) *Smile*
   Solution: With all phases of competition, it's important to remember to *smile*. As you practice your swimsuit walk,

practice smiling at the same time. Each time you practice, act as if you're competing.

5.) *Eye contact*
Solution: Again, practice makes perfect. When practicing walking and smiling at the same time, practice good eye contact as well.

Talent

1.) *Presentation and choreography*
Solution: Judges will be scoring you based partly on your presentation. If your movements are stiff and/or limited, points will be deducted. Judges will expect your performance to be smooth, so practice, practice, practice!

2.) *Projection*
Solution: How you project yourself to the judging panel and the audience is a crucial part of your talent presentation. If you are timid in your on-stage movements, fail to sing out, or don't perform your piece with enthusiasm, it will hurt your scores. Be confident!

3.) *Vocal, dance and instrumental errors*
Solution: Being nervous can greatly affect one's performance. Although some contestants are able to handle stage fright better than others, nerves can be a key factor in mistakes during a contestant's talent presentation. Missed notes, or missed steps in a talent performance do stand out, and will cost you points. Practicing your piece over and over until it becomes a part of you will give you more confidence, and doing it on stage will be relatively easy.

4.) *Costuming*
Solution: The outfit you wear for talent is almost as important as what you will be performing. The outfit that you wear helps accentuate your presentation. You want judges

and the audience to really get involved in your performance. Choosing an outfit that relates to your piece is essential in getting them involved and making your presentation more enjoyable.

5.) *Smile and eye contact*
Solution: If you are singing or dancing, it's important to make as much eye contact as possible. If you are playing the piano, or another type of instrument, looking at the judges frequently is not always appropriate. The mood of your piece also affects whether or not you should smile at the judges during your presentation. By consulting with your dance or voice coach, or your music instructor, he/she will be able to give you valuable pointers on facial expression, as this is an important part of your presentation.

Evening Gown

Some pageants include an on-stage question during the evening gown competition. If you will have an on-stage question, it may be one the director gives you prior to competition. Or, you may have a question that is based on your platform or current events. For this reason it's important to keep up with the news and have a thorough knowledge of your platform.

Your question may be one that is given spontaneously by the emcee. Again, practicing at home by answering questions posed to you by your family and friends is one of the best ways to practice.

In evening gown, you will also be judged on the fit of your gown, how the style and color looks on you, your walk, and the way you smile and maintain eye contact with the judges.

In conclusion, remember that earning high scores in a pageant isn't easy, but it's a lot easier if you know what the judges will be looking for.

Chapter 8 – The Competition

Chapter 8
The Competition

Pageant weekend will arrive in a flurry of excitement and anxiety. You'll look back on all the hours you've spent getting ready for the big moment and think with a sense of panic that all that time may not have been enough. Even though you know you're ready, you will probably have moments when you feel unprepared.

As competition time draws near, and you prepare to leave for the pageant, it's important to get off to a solid start. That brings us to a subject that no contestant enjoys, but every contestant has to do it: pack luggage. As you pull your suitcases out of the closet, think about the things you will need to bring with you. Jot them down, making a written list of every item. If you pack haphazardly, you'll forget something. Then when you arrive at the pageant and realize what you've forgotten, you'll be stressed. It may be something small like a toothbrush, but you may not have the opportunity to leave and buy a new one. And, a weekend without a toothbrush is not a good weekend, no matter how you place in the pageant.

As you pack, here are a few tips:

1.) Whether you realize it or not, your purse is your smallest "suitcase." Before you begin packing things in your other pieces of luggage, make sure that your purse contains a calling card (in case of an emergency), and other important forms of identification (some pageants now ask to see i.d. or a copy of your birth certificate upon registering). If you have a cellular phone and will be driving a long distance, don't forget to put an extra battery in your purse.

2.) Before you pack, make sure that your luggage is clearly labeled with your name, address, and phone number. If you're staying in a hotel where someone will be bringing your luggage up to you, the last thing you want is to have your luggage sent to the wrong room or get misplaced. Having your bags marked helps prevent this from happening.

3.) When you begin packing, you should first pack any medication that you may need. If you have asthma and need to bring an inhaler, or if you have any other type of medical condition, packing these items first will keep you from leaving them behind.

4.) If you're wearing contact lenses, be sure to bring all of your cleaning solutions with you, such as your contact case and saline/cleaning solution. If you have a pair of glasses, bring those as well. You can wear them when you're in your room during evening hours to give your eyes a break from wearing your contact lenses.

5.) Try to minimize as much as possible. During pageant weekend, you may find yourself having to carry around your own luggage. If that's the case, you don't want to be carrying around several suitcases. Pack only what you will need.

6.) To help minimize what you take with you, purchase trial size items of the health and beauty products you need (if you are required to be at the pageant for several days this may not be possible). Packing regular size bottles of shampoo and conditioner only takes up more space in your suitcase, and they are heavy. Trial size products come in virtually every brand and are inexpensive.

7.) An item frequently forgotten by contestants is shoes. The contestant will have packed her evening gown shoes but will have forgotten her shoes that go with her interview suit. Try packing a bag in which you put only your shoes. By doing this, it keeps you from forgetting a certain pair. It also saves you the time of shuffling through to the bottom of your suitcase looking for the right pair. Plus, after wearing shoes for an activity, the last thing you want to do is put them back into

Think of the things you will need to pack for competition, then make a written list. This will keep you from forgetting important items that you will need for the pageant.

a suitcase with your clothes. And, out of consideration for your roommate, you also don't want to have your shoes lined up all around your room, or taking up the entire closet. When packing your shoes, be sure to include a pair that goes with everything. You never know when a heel or strap may break and you'll need a spare pair.

8.) As you pack your shoes, don't forget to pack at least 4-5 pairs of nude colored panty hose. In the hustle and bustle of getting ready for each event, it's hard not to tear a run in your stockings (especially if you're wearing long nails).

9.) As you begin to pack your clothing, remember to pack all of your hanging clothes (such as your competition clothing and any other items you want to keep from getting wrinkled) in a hanging/garment bag. Just in case, bring a small iron with you. Even in a garment bag, your clothes may get slightly wrinkled.

Dressing for Success

The clothes you wear to the different pageant activities are almost as important as the clothes you wear in competition. Arriving at the pageant or attending a pageant activity dressed inappropriately is a big mistake. Remember you are competing for a chance to be a preliminary, state, or national titleholder. You need to look the part all the time.

Your director should be able to help you choose which outfits to bring along. If you don't have a director to help you, ask other contestants who have competed in the pageant before for their opinion on what clothing you should bring.

Arrival/Registration

Check-in time is fun even though you may feel a little nervous. Registration is also when you will get a first glimpse of who your fellow competitors will be.

When you arrive to register, be organized, having items with you that pageant personnel may ask for, such as identification, ticket money, or any remaining sponsor fees that need to be paid.

But again, enjoy every moment from the time you check in until the time you leave. This is a once in a lifetime experience and it will pass quickly.

Activities

The number of, and type of, activities you participate in during a pageant depends on the pageant, its director, and where the event is being held.

As mentioned before, dress appropriately for each activity. Some pageants will let the judges watch contestants during activities, so you always want to be prepared. Regardless of whether or not the judges are watching, "looking the part" of a preliminary, state, or national winner will help you maintain your confidence throughout the pageant weekend.

Dress Rehearsal

Learning an opening number can be a big source of stress during pageant weekend. Some girls can pick up dance moves easily, while others find it hard not to step on their own toes.

Arrive at the dress rehearsal in whatever the pageant personnel asks you to bring, and have an open mind. Don't get easily frustrated with yourself if you don't pick up the routine right away. Just do your best and it will all come together. In your spare time, practice the number with some of your fellow contestants. This will not only help you learn the routine, but will also help you make friends with other contestants.

Before the Pageant

As the starting time for the pageant approaches, go over in your mind the things you will need to bring with you to the theatre or auditorium. Unlike when you packed for the pageant, if you forget something you need to take to the pageant you won't have an opportunity to go and get it later. You may want to have someone help you get your things together before you leave, as nerves can cause you to become forgetful.

Competition Time

I believe that the toughest moments are the ones not during competition, but before competition. Anxieties rise as the starting time approaches. But once you start going through the motions of the opening number, you'll feel your nervousness dwindle as you get caught up in concentrating on your perfor-

When you're on stage, don't forget the three "p's": poise, personality, and projection.

mance and being on stage.

As you go through the evening, stay focused on the three "P's":

Poise

Judges don't expect you to be perfect, but you need to come as close to perfection as possible. One important factor in doing this is to maintain good poise. Execute your turns neatly and make sure your walk looks smooth. Your arms should move gracefully and not be swinging, or look stiff.

Personality

Throughout the competition, don't become so preoccupied with your performance that you lose your personality. Maintain good eye contact and remember to smile, smile, smile! Remember to let the judges see the real you.

Projection

While on stage, maintain your confidence so that it projects not only to the judges but the audience. Work the judging panel and the audience so that you take control of the stage and they become involved in your performance.

Throughout the pageant, stay focused. Don't worry about how well other contestants appear to be scoring. Don't look at the pageant in its entirety, instead, take it one phase at a time. Concentrate on giving each area of competition your best. After you finish one phase, put it behind you and think about the next portion of the pageant. You'll be surprised at how quickly the night will go by. Before you realize it, you'll be lined up on stage, anxiously awaiting the final results.

Chapter 9 – Learning to Lose

Chapter 9
Learning to Lose

As mentioned before, there have been contestants who have won preliminary, state and national titles all on their first try. But instances like this are not the norm. Upon speaking with state and national titleholders you'll find that many of them tried several times to win a title. Unfortunately, one of the lessons many contestants have to learn in pageantry is that if you want to win, you must first learn to lose.

Should you enter a pageant and not win, it's normal to feel disappointed, discouraged, and sometimes even a little angry. After months of preparation, all of your hard work came to a climax and was over in a few hours. Most of your time on stage seemed like a whirlwind, and after the results were announced, you found yourself wondering what went wrong.

But it's in those minutes after the pageant that contestants make the biggest mistakes. They miss out on valuable opportunities because they are upset about not winning.

As hard as it is, you have to go against your emotions, because taking the time to follow these tips can help prevent you from losing other pageants in the future.

Don't Be A Sore Loser

As a director, I have seen numerous contestants make this mistake. They will get upset and angry — sometimes before they've even exited the stage. They'll go back to the dressing room and talk negatively about fellow contestants, the pageant, the judges, and the director. By acting this way the contestant only succeeds in accomplishing two things: 1.) They gain a bad reputation among people in the pageant industry. 2.) They lose out on any opportunity they may have had to be friends with any of the other contestants. Then, if you decide to enter another competition, your reputation will follow you. You'll soon notice that fellow contestants will keep their distance, and unfortunately the director may do the same. Remember, your reputation is invaluable. Being a sore loser will always work toward your disadvantage.

Consult with the Judges

After the pageant, ask the judges what they think your strong points and weak points were. Don't be afraid to ask them questions afterwards, as this is important in helping you know what you need to work on for future competitions. Most judges are happy to talk with contestants after the pageant, as they realize that their evaluations are important to helping a contestant reach their maximum potential.

Take Time to Unwind

One of the best things a contestant can do after the competition and its festivities are over, is to go back to the hotel room and relax. Take a break and try to get the pageant off your mind. Don't go over in your mind areas in which you think you failed, because no matter how many pageants you do, none of your performances will ever be flawless. Everyone makes mistakes. There will always be something you feel you could have said or done differently.

Also, wait a few days before you look at the pageant video and critique your performance. After some time has passed you'll be able to look at the competition and your performance more objectively.

Talk with Your Director

A few days after the pageant, call your director and ask for your scores. Seeing your scores will give you a better idea of how you placed overall and will also enable you to learn which areas were strong and which need improvement. When you call for your scores, ask your director what he/she thought kept you from winning the title. Your director should be able to give you valuable advice about your performance.

Asking the Tough Question

After you have taken time to relax, you will ultimately have to ask yourself the question: "Do I want to compete again?"

If the answer is "no," is it just because you didn't win the title, or is it because you realize that competing in pageants is not for you.

If you answered negatively because you didn't win the title, then you may want to reconsider competing in the future. If your perception of whether or not you enjoyed the competition is based on winning, then the more pageants you enter and fail to win, the more you'll make your life miserable. As mentioned before, losing is often a part of winning. You have to be willing to take that chance if you want to compete.

If you didn't enjoy competing because you realized that participating in a pageant was not what you thought it would be, you're not the first to make this discovery. Pageants aren't for everyone. Deciding you don't want to compete again doesn't mean you failed, it just means you have different interests. Some girls will compete in pageants because their parents, friends, or their boyfriend, wants them to. Each time pageant weekend comes, the contestant finds herself going through the motions of competing, the whole time wanting to be somewhere else. If pageants aren't your forte, discuss with those who want you to enter the reasons why you don't want to compete. The sooner you quit competing and find other interests that you enjoy, the better off you'll be.

Starting Again

There are some contestants who don't have to ask themselves whether or not they want to compete again. Almost immediately after the competition, they're ready to try another pageant. For some girls it may take a little longer, but the desire to compete is there, and within a few weeks they find themselves looking for another pageant to enter.

One reason you may have lost the previous competition was because it may not have fit your particular style. Earlier I mentioned the difference between glitz vs. conservative pageants. You may have felt that the pageant was the type of competition you wanted to enter, but as you went through the competition you realized that it wasn't your style. Or, one of the judges may have suggested you try another system. Whatever the case may be, begin looking for other pageants to enter. Don't be afraid to try another pageant system. As mentioned before, if you want to succeed in pageantry you have to find the pageant system that's right for you.

As you prepare for your next competition, remember that preparing for your first pageant took a lot of hard work. Even though you have a "solid base" to start from going into your second competition, there's still work that needs to be done. As mentioned earlier, review what suggestions the judges gave you in your previous pageant. Also, go over your scores, comments from the director, and review the pageant's video (if one is available). Pull all of these things together and begin preparing again, as you did before. As always, pace yourself, giving adequate time to do the work that's needed, instead of trying to cram it in at the last minute.

While you get ready for the next competition, try not to fall into the trap that some contestants do. Often a contestant will try to become a carbon copy of the person she lost to in the previous competition. She will assume that since that person won, copying her exact style and look will help her win her next competition. Although you can learn from the winner's performance, you have to implement her strong points into your style, not become her "clone."

Another error that some girls make is that after they lose a pageant, they make radical changes when preparing for their next competition. They will get a new fitness trainer, quit working with their pageant coach (or get a new one), and make drastic changes to their wardrobe. If your trainer has had experience working with pageant contestants, your coach is qualified, and you had an experienced sales clerk help you choose your wardrobe, you shouldn't have to make big changes. Although the judges may have made some minor suggestions, if you went about preparing the correct way you shouldn't have to do a complete overhaul with your presentation and performance. Remember, it's important to stick with people who are experienced in preparing girls for competition the right way. They're hard to find and if you have a group working with you who knows about pageantry, it's to your advantage to keep working with them.

Showtime

When pageant time arrives, focus on this competition only. Don't think about what happened in your previous pageant. Concentrate on doing your best in each phase of this competition. Make it a pleasurable experience, and go into it with a desire to win.

Chapter 10 – Representing Your Title

Chapter 10
Representing Your Title

You're standing on stage beneath the bright glare of the stage lights. The announcer begins to call the name of the fourth runner-up, third runner-up, and second runner-up. Then, there's a pause. The crowd starts to cheer and you hear members of the audience yell out the name of their favorite contestant. Within seconds, you hear the name of the first runner-up, followed quickly by your name being announced as the winner. Suddenly, roses are pushed into your arms, the former queen hurriedly places the crown on your head, and fellow contestants rush to give you congratulatory hugs. It all takes place within a matter of minutes, but it's those minutes that will change your life forever.

While you were preparing for the competition by exercising regularly and resisting those chocolate cravings so that you could fit into your swimsuit, there were times when you probably asked yourself: "Was it a mistake to enter this pageant?" Now, walking down the runway with your new title and waving to the crowd, you realize the hard work *was* worth it. But as you finish your walk down the runway, little do you realize that there's more hard work that lies ahead.

Becoming A Role Model

When you win your title, you become a role model to many young girls. Some pageant winners think that role model status is reserved for state or national winners only. Not so. With any title, whether it be at the preliminary, state, or national level, you become someone that people admire.

I was reminded of this when I accompanied one of my winners to an appearance. I watched as a young girl stared at my winner for several seconds before she quickly tapped her on the shoulder and shyly said hello. I don't think that my winner had any idea how much this young girl admired her, but situations like this happen frequently when you become a pageant winner.

As always, the best advice I can give to titleholders is to be themselves wherever they go. Remember that there is always someone watching you to see how you handle different situations. Don't put undue pressure on yourself to be perfect, no one expects that and you shouldn't either. But being a titleholder is a job, and with that comes the responsibility of being someone who others admire. That means taking time for that extra photograph and getting up early to make it to an appearance when you really feel like sleeping in.

Personal Appearances

From the moment you are crowned, you begin the fun, and sometimes challenging task, of representing your title. Everywhere you go you not only represent yourself, but also the pageant organization, and, as mentioned above, wherever you go, people will consider you a role model.

Some pageant winners will wait until after a state or national competition to begin scheduling appearances, while others will schedule appearances almost immediately after being crowned.

Sometimes pageant directors will plan your appearances for you, while others will allow you to keep track of your appearances and appointments. Regardless of who is doing your scheduling, one of your first purchases as a titleholder should be to buy a daily planner. This planner will enable you to jot down all of your appointments, thus helping you avoid the embarrassment of not showing up for a function because you forgot to write it down. Planners come in a variety of sizes, but getting one that fits in your purse is your best option. This way you will always have it with you in case of an emergency.

When scheduling appointments, jot down the following information:

1.) The name and number of the contact person who is coordinating the event
2.) The exact time you need to arrive (sometimes a group will want you to arrive a few minutes early for photos) and the time the event is scheduled to end
3.) What type of clothing you need to wear (casual, semiformal, formal)
4.) Whether or not you need to bring or wear your crown and sash
5.) Detailed directions (Never assume that you will make it to a function in time if you've never been to the location. Doing this could cause you to be late and would make you and the pageant system you represent look unprofessional.) Before you leave for a function you may want to bring a photo/autograph pad or stack of photos with you. You'll be asked to sign many autographs during your reign, so it's a good idea to stock up on photos. Your director should be able to give you the names of companies who print autograph pads or large quantity duplicates of photos. Pageant magazines also list the names of companies who specialize in this type work.

Once you arrive at the event, you'll see that people perceive the pageant by the way you represent it. Representing the pageant well can cause individuals and businesses who come in contact with you to want to sponsor the pageant by donating gift packages and prizes towards next year's competition. This will speak well of you and help not only the pageant but your successor.

If your pageant provides you with business cards, distribute them as much as possible, as this helps get your name and the pageant's name out among the different communities.

Platforms and Community Service

Some pageants require titleholders to have a platform issue that they promote during their year of reign. This is an issue

Winning a title gives you many opportunities to develop your public speaking skills.

that can be on a topic of your choice. The majority of speaking engagements and appearances you have during your year may come from civic groups and organizations that want you to come and speak about your platform, so it's important to know about the issue you're promoting.

When selecting a platform, choose a topic that's of interest to you. Often titleholders will choose an issue that's popular, but it isn't a topic they can relate to. The most effective type of platform is one that has a special meaning for you. You'll be able to promote the issue more effectively if it's something that you can put your heart into.

If the pageant system that you are representing requires the titleholder to have a platform issue, your director should be able to help you in developing a platform. He/she should be able to assist you in getting information about your platform, obtaining promotional information on your platform that you can take with you to appearances, and obtaining names and telephone numbers of people and/or groups that you can speak to about your platform issue. (If you are scheduling your own appearances, looking through your local phone book should give you some ideas on who you can call to set up speaking engagements.)

The biggest advantage of having a platform and being able to promote it within your community or state, is that you get to use your title toward helping other people. Whether it's helping an organization raise funds, providing special entertainment for an activity, or just volunteering where a group needs you most, you'll see that participating in community service is one of the most rewarding experiences that you'll ever have. Another advantage of community service is that it helps develop your interpersonal skills. This will help you tremendously at a state or national competition. When the competition arrives, you will have gained so much confidence from making public appearances and interacting with others, that it will show. It will help you feel more at ease in front of a judging panel and when you're on stage.

Preparing for State and National Competition

If your title was a preliminary to a state or national competition, you'll soon find that the steps you took for preliminary competition will start all over again, this time on a more intense level. Your schedule will be busy with photo shoots and fittings for your new pageant wardrobe. Your physical workouts will probably also become more frequent, as you continue to work with your trainer, or the trainer that your director has chosen for you.

As you prepare for the next level of competition, one of the biggest advantages is that you will have a director that can work with you on more of a one-on-one basis. You'll be able to benefit from his/her expertise which will make life much easier at the state or national competition.

My best advice to new titleholders is to be open to any suggestions your director may give you. Don't develop the attitude that because you have won a title you now know everything there is to know about pageants. Remember, your director has been to state and national competitions before, preparing girls for this particular type of competition. He/she knows what the judges will be looking for and how to prepare you accordingly. However, if your director is pushing you in a direction you feel uncomfortable, let him/her know. Be honest with them from the beginning. If you aren't, you'll make yourself miserable and it will show, especially in the attitude you have toward representing your title.

Another suggestion I have for new titleholders is to try not to lose your identity. It's your uniqueness that stood out among other competitors and helped you win the title. Among the busy schedule and the new attention you've been receiving, it's easy to lose sight of who you are. Try to take time out each day to refocus and get away from it all. This will help you return to your "pageant duties" refreshed and with a new attitude. It's a good way to prevent you from getting burned out and will also make your year's reign a more enjoyable experience.

Arriving at the Top

For many girls, winning a preliminary title that enables them to advance to a state or national competition is a dream come true. For other contestants the thought of advancing to a higher level of competition was something they hadn't thought a lot about. But once the realization hits you that you are going to be competing at the state or national level within a few weeks or months, it will be one of the most exciting moments you've ever experienced.

When you arrive at the state or national competition, you'll be immersed in a variety of activities. From morning until evening you'll be involved in dress rehearsals, photo shoots, and taking sight-seeing tours with fellow contestants. While you're involved in these activities, try to make friends with your fellow competitors. Being able to make new friends with the other girls you will meet is one of the biggest rewards that pageants have to offer.

When you arrive at the state or national pageant, and as you go through pageant week, your goal is to win the overall title. Although many girls will claim they go to state or nationals with no expectation other than to have a good time, I think every contestant would love to walk away with the overall title. But when the time comes to compete, don't put too much pressure on yourself. All you can do is be yourself and give it your absolute best. As you will soon notice, the competition you face at the state or national level will be much stiffer than what you encountered in your preliminary pageant.

As you compete, keep in mind three things: 1.) *Listen to your director.* As mentioned previously he/she has been to this level of competition before, and will know how to guide you through it. 2.) *Stay focused by concentrating on each phase of competition as it arrives.* For example, you will make mistakes in interview if you are worrying about your evening gown question. Looking at all phases of competition and grouping them together in your mind will cause you to be extremely nervous. Take it one step at a time. 3.) *If you don't win the overall title, accept it and move on.* Often, contestants let themselves fall into depression if they don't win the overall title. They let themselves believe that because they did not win the overall title they were a disappointment to their director, their sponsors, and their family and friends. Don't let this happen to you. Every director, your sponsors, and your family and friends, realize how tough state and national competition can be. They understand that there are no guarantees. Be happy with the fact that you were able to compete at that level, as many girls will never have that opportunity, and don't let not winning the competition negatively affect your self-esteem.

Life After the Crown

Your year as a titleholder will go by quickly. Before you realize it, it will be time to crown your successor.

When pageant week (or weekend) arrives you will have the fun opportunity of being the reigning state queen. Contestants vying for your title will be asking you for lots of pageant advice and you may be asked to do some interviews with the local media.

As you see the contestants with their pre-pageant jitters, you'll soon realize that being the reigning queen during pageant week is more enjoyable and a lot less stressful than competing.

But as you place the crown on the new winner, you'll be surprised at how quickly the attention will turn from you to her. Although you'll be happy for your successor, you may feel a touch of sadness when you see her making her walk down the runway. Having emotions such as this is perfectly normal. For the last twelve months you've worked hard at representing the title, and now you have to let it go. But there is life after the crown, and just because you're no longer a reigning queen, doesn't mean you have to lose contact with the pageant industry. There are many opportunities that come with being a former pageant winner. Here are a few of them:

Personal Appearances

Just because you have given up your title doesn't mean that you won't be asked to make any more personal appearances. You'll be surprised to find that many organizations will want you to come and speak. If, during your year of reign you worked with an organization that was related to your platform, they will more than likely be happy to have you continue to work with them. You may want to send those who invited you to make appearances and speaking engagements a letter telling them that you're still interested in being involved in their activities, and also let them know in the letter if you have a new address or phone number since relinquishing your title.

Judging

As a former pageant winner, you may be asked by other pageants to serve as a judge. Serving as a judge can help you keep up with current pageant trends, should you be considering the option of competing again.

Coaching

Coaching is another benefit that comes with being a former titleholder. Because of the experience you gained during your reign, girls who are interested in winning a title will want to come to you for pageant coaching. Some former pageant winners have been asked by so many contestants to coach, that they have opened their own pageant consultation business.

If pageant consulting is of interest to you, one of the first decisions you will need to make is whether or not to charge for your services. If you do want to charge a fee, you may want to talk with other pageant coaches to see how much they charge for consultations and what type of consulting is included in that fee. Consulting with other coaches will keep you from undercharging or overcharging for your services.

If you decide to start a pageant consultation business, consider having business cards made to distribute at pageants and formal wear stores. This is an excellent way to promote your name and company within the pageant industry.

Becoming A Director

Some former pageant winners enjoy pageantry so much that they will decide to make it a year round job by becoming a director. Whether or not it's at the preliminary, state, or national level, there are a variety of positions open should you want to try your hand at being a director. Pageant magazines which are devoted to the pageant industry often contain advertisements placed by pageant organizations who are looking for directors, but you may choose to start your own pageant system. Being a director is both a rewarding and challenging position. Talking with your former director will give you some valuable insight on whether or not a director's position is right for you.

Contact Information

If you have never competed in a pageant before, and are looking for ways to get local pageant information, the following is a list of businesses and organizations that typically carry the names and numbers of local pageants and pageant directors:

Chamber of Commerce
Visitor's Centers
Newspapers
Television/Radio Stations
Bridal & Formal Wear stores

By calling a pageant's national office, you can also obtain information about when your state's pageant is held, state and preliminary directors, and state preliminaries.

Once you begin competing, you will hear fellow contestants recommend pageants to enter, and they are usually happy to give you the names and numbers of those conducting those pageants.

Final Thoughts

As you've read this book, I hope that you have gained valuable insight on what it takes to win a pageant and how to represent a title effectively.

Competing in pageants offers girls and young women so many opportunities. From nurturing self-esteem, to winning scholarships, the rewards of competing in pageants are immeasurable.

Good luck to each of you! I wish you the best!

The Author

About the Author

Shana Gammon graduated from Liberty University with a degree in Journalism in 1994. She is currently the Director of the Miss Festival of Virginia, a state pageant that she started in 1996. Her pageant judges have included former national winners from the Miss USA and Miss Teen USA systems and former and reigning state queens from the Miss America, Miss USA and Miss Teen USA pageants. She resides in Lynchburg with her husband, Chuck, and her daughter, Gabrielle. You can write to the author at: Shana Gammon, P.O. Box 126, Lynchburg, VA 24505. Or, you can e-mail her at: watchingthewinners@juno.com.